We Love ID-UL-ADHA

Alice Green

WAYLAND

D0537432

60000216785

Published in 2012 by Wayland

Hachette Children's Books
338 Euston Road, London NW1 3BH

© Copyright 2007 Wayland

The right of Alice Green to be identified as
the author of the work has been asserted by her
in the Copyright, Designs and Patents Act 1988.

All rights reserved.

Produced for Wayland by Q2A Media
Series Editor: Jean Coppendale
Senior Design Manager: Simmi Sikka
Designer: Diksha Khatri
Consultant: Marilyn Bowes

A catalogue record for this book is available from
the British Library

ISBN 978 0 7502 6880 6

Printed in China

First published in 2007 by Wayland

This paperback edition published by Wayland in 2012

Wayland is a division of Hachette Children's Books,
an Hachette UK company.
www.hachette.co.uk

Northamptonshire
Libraries & Information
Services
NW

Askews & Holts	

The publishers would like to thank the following for
allowing us to reproduce their pictures in this book:

Corbis: title page, 20, Studio DL; 13, Christine Osborne; 9,
Kazuyoshi Nomachi / Alamy: 4, 23, Charles O. Cecil / Ali
Abbas: 5 / Photolibrary: 6, Photo Researchers, Inc. /
REUTERS: 7, Aladin Abdel Naby; 8, Crack Palinggi; 11, Ali
Jarekji; 15, Bazuki Muhammad; 21, Ajay Verma / EPA: 10 /
THE HINDU: cover, 12, 19, 22, 14, / Alexander Boden: 16
/ Islamic Relief: 17 / wildphotos.com: 18, Anil Dev.

Contents

Happy Id!

Id-ul-Adha is one of the most important Muslim festivals. It is celebrated two months after Id-ul-Fitr, a festival which comes at the end of **Ramadan**, the month when Muslims **fast** through each day.

Children and men from Oman, in the Middle East, wearing traditional clothes on a picnic during Id-ul-Adha.

Id-ul-Adha also marks the end of **Hajj**. This is a journey, or pilgrimage, which Muslims make to their holy city of Makkah in Saudi Arabia.

Hajj pilgrims visit the Sacred Mosque in Makkah.

DID YOU KNOW?

Id-ul-Adha is also known as Hari Raya Aidiladha in Indonesia and Malaysia. In Turkey, Muslims call it Kurban Bayrami.

A story of sacrifice

Boys read the Holy **Qur'an** on Id-ul-Adha. The Qur'an contains the story of Ibrahim ﷺ and Ishmail.

Ibrahim ﷺ is one of the **prophets** of Islam. Muslims believe that Allah (the Muslim name for God) appeared to Ibrahim ﷺ in a dream and asked him to **sacrifice** his son, Ishmail, to show his obedience to Allah. Ibrahim ﷺ followed Allah's orders and took Ishmail to Mina, a city near Makkah.

Women in Cairo, Egypt, pray during Id-ul-Adha. Men and women pray in separate places – some women pray in their homes.

Just as Ibrahim ﷺ prepared to offer his son, Allah stopped him. It is Ibrahim's ﷺ obedience to Allah that Muslims celebrate every year at Id-ul-Adha.

Sacred pilgrimage

The festival of Id-ul-Adha takes place on the last day of Hajj. During Hajj, Muslims travel the same path that Ibrahim ﷺ took to Mina to sacrifice Ishmail.

These Indonesian pilgrims are flying to Makkah for the Hajj.

Millions of Muslims arrive at Makkah about nine days before Id-ul-Adha. When they get there, they have to do certain things. These include walking around the **Ka'bah**, a large square-shaped building in the middle of the Sacred Mosque in Makkah.

The Ka'bah, in the centre of this picture, is the holiest building for Muslims. They believe that it was built by Ibrahim ﷺ and Ishmail.

DID YOU KNOW?

Muslims always face the direction of the Ka'bah when they pray.

End of the pilgrimage

Throughout Hajj, Muslim men wear special white clothes. This is so they all look the same before Allah.

On the tenth and final day of Hajj, Muslims gather at Mina for their last duty. The pilgrims begin the day by throwing pebbles at the Jamarah, a stone pillar that stands for the devil.

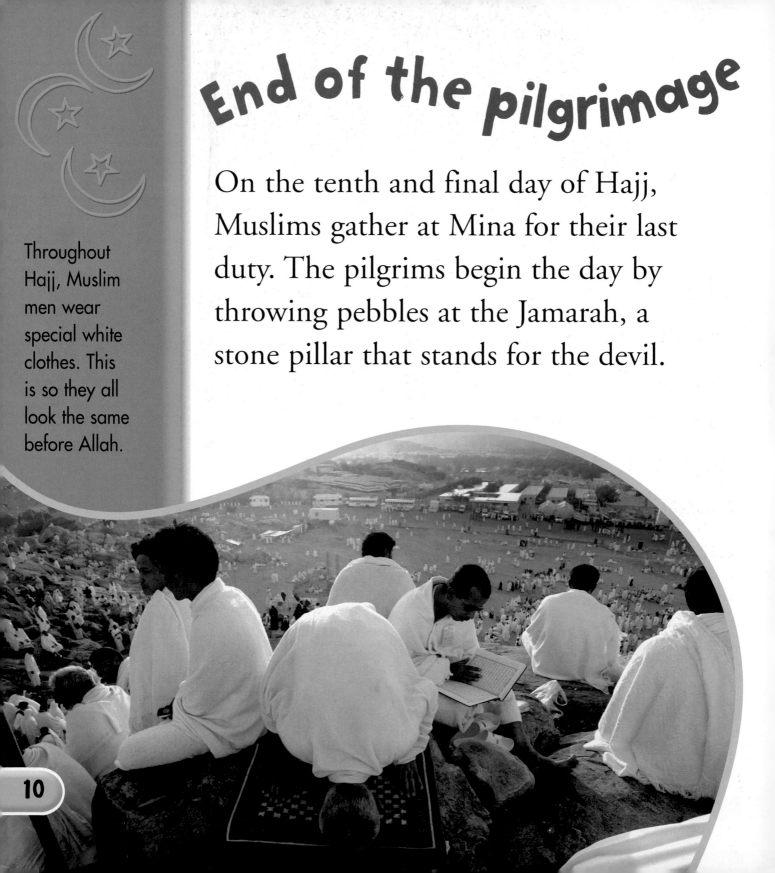

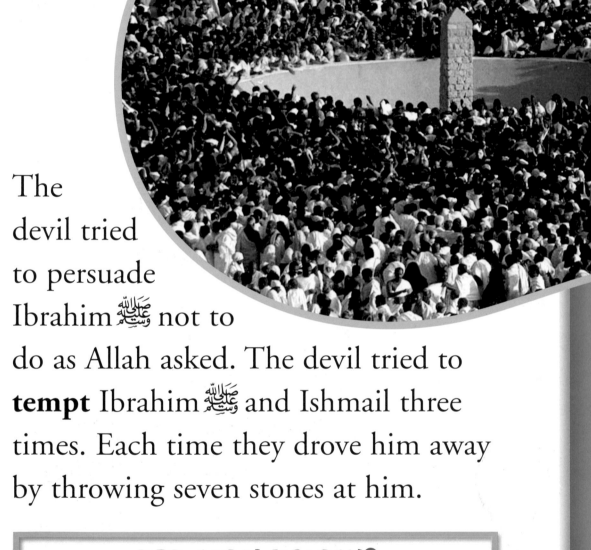

The devil tried to persuade Ibrahim ﷺ not to do as Allah asked. The devil tried to **tempt** Ibrahim ﷺ and Ishmail three times. Each time they drove him away by throwing seven stones at him.

Muslims gather at the Jamarah pillar to throw their stones.

DID YOU KNOW?

Muslims believe that the Jamarah pillar stands on the spot where the devil appeared before Ibrahim ﷺ.

11

Visit to a mosque

On the day of Id-ul-Adha, Muslims around the world who are not on Hajj wake up early and put on new clothes. Then they gather at a mosque to join in morning prayers.

Muslims offering Id-ul-Adha prayers at Moti Masjid, in Bhopal, India.

A **mu'adhin**, from a mosque in Cairo, Egypt, calls Muslims to prayer.

Id-ul-Adha is a time when Muslims ask Allah to forgive their sins, and to help them become kinder and stronger.

13

Exchanging greetings

After prayers, Muslims hug and greet each other. Then they visit family and friends, and celebrate the festival of Id-ul-Adha together.

Two boys in Patna, India, greet each other on Id-ul-Adha.

A Malaysian boy pours rose water onto his mother's grave on Id-ul-Adha.

Many Muslims also take time to visit **cemeteries** and pray for their family and friends who have died.

15

Feast of Sacrifice

Id-ul-Adha teaches the importance of looking after each other and obeying Allah. Many Muslims buy meat from special shops and give some of it to the poor.

Muslims in London buy meat from shops like this one on Id-ul-Adha.

Food being given to the poor during Id-ul-Adha in California, USA.

Muslims make sure that no one is hungry on this special day. The pilgrims in Makkah also give out food and money among poor pilgrims.

Delicious feast

Muslims make delicious food as a part of the Id-ul-Adha celebrations. Different kinds of food are made by Muslims around the world.

A boy enjoys a bowl of sweet pudding prepared specially on Id-ul-Adha.

A feast of biryani and kebabs.

Biryani, a dish made with rice and lamb, is a favourite with lots of children in India. Many Indonesian Muslims make rice cakes that are eaten with lamb or chicken curry.

DID YOU KNOW?

The Muslims of Oman, in the Middle East, make a special sweet dish called halwa. It is made of wheat, sugar and almonds.

children's delight

Part of Id-ul-Adha is also a children's festival. Many children receive presents from their family and friends.

A Malaysian mother gives her son money on Id-ul-Adha.

An Indian father buys balloons for his son.

Many Muslim parents take their children out on picnics or to amusement parks. The children spend the day having fun.

DID YOU KNOW?

Some Muslims living in Rehaniya, Israel, give coins to all the children in the village on this day.

Colourful celebrations

Some Muslims spend Id-ul-Adha outdoors. Many go shopping for sweets and presents for their friends and relatives.

People in Srinagar, India, shop for Id-ul-Adha gifts.

In some countries, such as Jordan and the United Arab Emirates, music and dance are an important part of the celebrations.

Children watch men perform a special dance as a part of the Id-ul-Adha celebrations in Al-Hamra, Oman.

23

Index and glossary

cemeteries special places where the dead are buried

fast to go without food or drink

Hajj the yearly pilgrimage, or journey, to Makkah, which all Muslims try to make at least once in their lives

Ka'bah a black, square-shaped structure built in the middle of the Great Mosque at Makkah

mu'adhin the person who calls Muslims to prayer from a mosque

prophets religious leaders who are thought to be messengers of God

Qur'an the holy book of Islam

Ramadan the month in the Islamic year when Muslims fast between sunrise and sunset

sacrifice to kill a person, or animal, as an offering to a god

tempt to try to make someone do something wrong by promising a reward in return